SandCastle

Word Families Set 7

-oon as in spoon

Carey Molter

Consulting Editor Monica Marx, M.A./Reading Specialist

ABDO
Publishing Company

Published by SandCastle™, an imprint of ABDO Publishing Company, 4940 Viking Drive, Edina, Minnesota 55435.

Printed in the United States.

Credits
Edited by: Pam Price
Curriculum Coordinator: Nancy Tuminelly
Cover and Interior Design and Production: Mighty Media
Photo Credits: Corbis Images, Digital Vision, Eyewire Images, Hemera, PhotoDisc

Library of Congress Cataloging-in-Publication Data

Molter, Carey, 1973-
    -Oon as in spoon / Carey Molter.
       p. cm. -- (Word families. Set VII)
    Summary: Introduces, in brief text and illustrations, the use of the letter combination "oon" in such words as "spoon," "moon," "raccoon," and "balloon."
    ISBN 1-59197-266-3
    1. Readers (Primary) [1. Vocabulary. 2. Reading.] I. Title. II. Series.

PE1119 .M628 2003
428.1--dc21   2002038219

SandCastle™ books are created by a professional team of educators, reading specialists, and content developers around five essential components that include phonemic awareness, phonics, vocabulary, text comprehension, and fluency. All books are written, reviewed, and leveled for guided reading, early intervention reading, and Accelerated Reader® programs and designed for use in shared, guided, and independent reading and writing activities to support a balanced approach to literacy instruction.

Let Us Know

After reading the book, SandCastle would like you to tell us your stories about reading. What is your favorite page? Was there something hard that you needed help with? Share the ups and downs of learning to read. We want to hear from you! To get posted on the ABDO Publishing Company Web site, send us e-mail at:

sandcastle@abdopub.com

SandCastle Level: Transitional

-oon Words

baboon

balloon

loon

noon

raccoon

spoon

The baboon climbs on its mom.

The balloon is in the sky.

The loon is in the water.

The clock says it's noon.

The raccoon is on the tree.

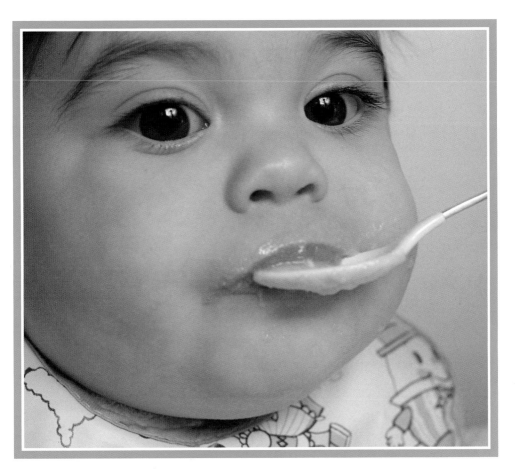

The baby eats from a
spoon.

Boon and Joon's Fun Afternoon

This is Boon.

Boon is a raccoon.

This is his pal Joon.

Joon is a baboon.

Joon and Boon
have lunch at noon.

Boon eats his soup
with a spoon.

Boon and Joon
watch a cartoon.

The cartoon is about
a loon and a goon.

Boon likes to croon.

Boon croons a tune
for Joon.

Boon and Joon ride
in a hot-air balloon.

Up, up, up to the moon!
What a fun afternoon!

The -oon Word Family

afternoon	moon
baboon	noon
balloon	raccoon
cartoon	soon
croon	spoon
goon	swoon
loon	

Glossary

Some of the words in this list may have more than one meaning. The meaning listed here reflects the way the word is used in the book.

afternoon   the part of the day from noon until evening

baboon   a large monkey with a long snout and big teeth

croon   to sing softly

goon   a stupid person

loon   a water bird that lives near lakes and can dive and swim under water

noon   twelve o'clock during the daytime

raccoon   a furry animal with rings on its tail and black markings on its face that look like a mask

About SandCastle™

A professional team of educators, reading specialists, and content developers created the SandCastle™ series to support young readers as they develop reading skills and stcategies and increase their general knowledge. The SandCastle™ series has four levels that correspond to early literacy development in young children. The levels are provided to help teachers and parents select the appropriate books for young readers.

Emerging Readers
(no flags)

Beginning Readers
(1 flag)

Transitional Readers
(2 flags)

Fluent Readers
(3 flags)

These levels are meant only as a guide. All levels are subject to change.

ABDO
Publishing Company

To see a complete list of SandCastle™ books and other nonfiction titles from ABDO Publishing Company, visit **www.abdopub.com** or contact us at:

4940 Viking Drive, Edina, Minnesota 55435 • 1-800-800-1312 • fax: 1-952-831-1632